NO HANG-UPS

JOHN CARFI & CLIFF CARLE

Illustrated by Paul Michael Davies

CCC Publications ● Los Angeles

Published by

CCC Publications
20306 Tau Place
Chatsworth, CA 91311

Copyright© 1983   Cliff Carle & John Carfi

Manufactured in the United States of America

Cover design & illustrations© 1984
CCC Publications

ISBN: 0-918259-00-2

First CCC Publications printing - March 1984
Second printing - September 1984
Third printing - January 1985
Fourth printing - March 1985
Fifth printing - June 1985
Sixth printing - October 1985
Seventh printing - December 1985
Eighth printing - January 1986
Ninth printing - June 1986
Tenth printing - August 1986
Eleventh printing - November 1986
Twelfth printing - March 1987
Thirteenth printing - July 1987
Fourteenth printing - August 1987
Fifteenth printing - October 1987
Sixteenth printing - January 1988
Seventeenth printing - June 1988
Eighteenth printing - August 1988
Nineteenth printing - March 1989
Twentieth printing - August 1989
Twenty-first printing - February 1990

ABOUT THE AUTHORS

CLIFF CARLE was born in Nebraska and now resides in Los Angeles, California where he is a comedian, comedy writer and a teacher of stand-up comedy. His other writings include a comedic screenplay, several TV comedy sketches and nightclub revues. Currently, he is finishing a book of humorous short stories. You might say Mr. Carle is not a somber kind of a guy.

JOHN CARFI was born in New Jersey and now lives in L.A. He makes his living as a stand-up comic, playing clubs from coast to coast. In addition, he both writes and teaches stand-up comedy. Generally, Mr. Carfi is a party person who loves fast cars, wild women and needlepoint.

ACKNOWLEDGMENT

We, the authors, wish to extend a special thanks to our business partner, Mark "Magic" Chutick, without whose diligent efforts this book would have been published a year earlier.

CONTENTS

–INTRODUCTION–

There seems to be two types of people in this world: those who own answering machines and those who have to leave messages on them. This book is written for both of you.

Perhaps the second most frustrating thing about owning an answering machine is playing back your day's messages only to hear a series of dial tones. (The first most frustrating thing is finding you forgot to turn it on.) Owners, this book just might prevent your machine from ending up in a garage sale—or the fast-rising sport of answering machine slam-dunking into garbage cans. After intensive testing on their own machines, the authors, two stand-up comedians, found that humorous or witty messages make it easier for callers to respond and <u>talk</u> <u>to</u> <u>a</u> <u>machine</u>. Of course, some people will not speak to a machine no matter how funny your message is—but you can often recognize them from their laugh or giggles.

Callers, after perusing this book, odds favor you'll find answering machines more fun and less intimidating. And you'll find it the perfect present for a friend who puts those messages on his machine that only a mother could love.

Therefore, hopes are, by the end of this book, everyone (owners and callers alike) will have NO HANG-UPS.

John Carfi
Cliff Carle

(NOTE ON MESSAGES: In fairness to both sexes, we have used the names "JANE" and "JOHN" arbitrarily. In most instances you'll be able to substitute your name and simply switch pronouns—<u>he</u> to <u>she</u>, or <u>her</u> to <u>his</u>, etc.)

JOKES AND PHONE FUN

Hello. I just bought a new answering machine and if you don't hang up, yours will be my first message. Now, if you finish your message too soon, don't worry—it happens to everyone now and then. And remember: the size of your message isn't important—it's your performance that counts.

BEEP...

Hi. You say answering machines give you a headache? Well, leave two messages, get plenty of sleep, and I'll call you in the morning.

BEEP. . .

This is Officer JOHN. You have the right to remain silent. If you speak, the message you leave can and will be used to call you back. If you do not have a message, the court will appoint you one.

BEEP. . .

JOHN here. Maybe you can help me out: I'm dating these two terrific girls, Kate and Edith. Kate is beautiful and a great cook. Edith is athletic and a great conversationalist. If I could have my way, they'd _both_ move in with me. But you know what they say: "You can't have your Kate and Edith too!"

BEEP. . .

Hello. This is JANE. You know, I make a lot of crude jokes, but I never make fun of the handicapped—because if it wasn't for them, I'd never get good parking spaces.

BEEP...

Hi. JANE here. Before you leave your message, I just want to mention that a friend of mine who lives in New York had to go to a specialist in San Francisco for a heart transplant. He just got back today—now there's a guy who <u>really</u> "left his heart in San Francisco!"

BEEP...

Hi. This is JOHN. I'm not answering my phone 'cuz I'm expecting an irate call. I got a bill from a creditor the other day. The guy was really mad! He wrote: "Get with it, Buddy, this bill is exactly one year old!" So I sent it back with a note: "Happy Birthday!"

BEEP...

Hello. This is JOHN. Leave a message at the tone and I'll get back to you—for those who don't have lips: 'eave a 'essage an' I 'all 'ou 'ack, 'ank 'ou!

BEEP. . .

(ROD SERLING IMITATION)
"You're dazed, bewildered, trapped in a world without time, where sound collides with color and shadows explode. You see a signpost up ahead—this is no ordinary telephone answering device. . . you have reached 'The Twilight Phone'."

BEEP. . .

(ANGRY)
Hi. I'm not home. I'm fed up and I'm going down to the local radio station to complain! You know how they always have those "Tests of the Emergency Broadcast System?" Well, what makes me angry is, at the end of the test, they never tell ya if ya passed!

BEEP...

Hello. I'm not in. I had to go to a funeral for this weird couple I used to know. It was kinda tragic! They froze to death at a Drive-In Movie. Yeah, they went to see "Closed For The Winter."

BEEP...

('VALLEY GIRL' VOICE)
Oh my God! I'm like, not in, you know? I'm shopping at this like, really gnarly mall. Anyway, like, leave a totally awesome message—but don't say anything grody, like barf me out! And remember, people who hang up are like, a total bummer, I'm sure. Gag me with a phone!

BEEP...

Hi. This is JANE. I had to rush down to the new Moron Bank. It's great! You deposit a toaster oven and they give you a thousand dollars!

BEEP...

(ADDING MACHINE IN BACKGROUND)
Last month my phone bill was $250.49! The month before that $189.30! This month it's $329.43! That averages out to about...89¢ a word! Whoever said talk is cheap???

BEEP...

(JUMP UP AND DOWN)
Hi. This is JOHN. I hope you can understand me. I have to keep jumping up and down. I just took some important medicine and forgot to read the label—it said, "Shake Well Before Using!"

BEEP...

Hello. This is JANE. Something's bothering me and I had to go have a talk with my pastor. Yesterday, in church, he told the congregation that we were put on Earth to help others. But he forgot to mention, why are the <u>others</u> here???

BEEP...

Hi. This is JOHN. I'm over at Manny Moron's house. Me and five other guys are helping him install a light bulb.

BEEP...

Hi. I went to visit an Oriental friend of mine who recently became a surgeon. He put himself through college by taking a job as a chef. Now don't get me wrong, I really like the guy, but I wouldn't want to have my appendix removed by a doctor who used to work at Benihana's.

BEEP...

Hi. I'm not in. I went out to see that new movie starring Bo Derrick, where she plays a schizophrenic—it's called "20."

BEEP...

Hi. This is JOHN. Well, as usual I'm at the Video Arcade. I can't believe how much money I've poured into those machines! You know, I wish I had a dime for every quarter I've spent!

BEEP...

If you're a friend and you got the money you owe me, just leave a message when you hear the mechanical tone. If you're a bill collector, please leave your name and number when you hear the...<u>dial</u> tone.

BEEP...

(SOAP OPERA VOICE)
"Hello. Welcome to <u>Phone</u> <u>Calls</u> <u>Of</u> <u>Our</u> <u>Lives.</u> Today, the life of JOHN and JANE and today's burning question: 'will they call back the strange people who called <u>them?</u>—or will they callously leave their friends on hold, as usual?' For the answer to these and other questions, leave a message at the tone."

BEEP...

Hello. This is JOHN. I won't be picking up. I'm in a strange mood today. I went to the doctor to have a mole removed from my back. But when I took off my shirt, he couldn't find it. He looked and looked but just couldn't find that mole! Oh well—must have been a <u>pigment</u> of my imagination.

BEEP...

Hi. I'm out trying to scrounge up a job. It's really getting bad. I went to the Unemployment Office today, but there was nobody available to help anyone. All the people who worked in the Unemployment Office were also on line.

BEEP. . .

(FIRM)
This is JANE! Leave a message at the tone—if you want—you don't have to—you are your own person—you do exactly what you want to do—it's your space. But do it right now—I'll call you as soon as I get back from my est meeting.

BEEP. . .

Hi. I'm not in. A friend of mine talked me into attending a forum on "Birth Control" with her. By the way, you ever notice that most people who favor birth control have already been born?

BEEP. . .

MESSAGES FOR FIVE
CONSECUTIVE DAYS:

Hello. This is JOHN. I'm taking off for a while, but before I go, I want to leave you with a very important message:

(1) Remember, wherever you go in life. . . there you are!

BEEP. . .

(2) Remember, you can lead a horse to water, but you can't make him. . .do a back-flip!

BEEP. . .

(3) Remember, never throw a piano into a coal mine. . .or you'll get A-flat miner!

BEEP. . .

(4) Remember, where there's a will. . . there's a dead person!

BEEP. . .

(5) Remember, never attempt suicide by drowning. . .if you can't swim!

BEEP. . .

BLAME IT ON YOUR RELATIVES!

This is JANE. I have to go to a funeral. My weird uncle drowned while skin diving—they found a Pepsi-Cola dispenser on his back.

BEEP. . .

Hi. I won't be in for a while. I had to take my wife to the doctor. She kissed our canary—now she has chirpees!

BEEP...

Hello. We're outside and won't hear the phone, so leave a message and we'll get back to you soon. We were kind of bored today and were going to go to the zoo and see the monkeys—then my brother-in-law showed up, so we didn't have to go.

BEEP...

Hi. I'm not home. I had to go visit my boring sister-in-law. The lady's kinda shallow—let me put it this way: if she were a swimming pool, you wouldn't even get your <u>knees</u> wet!

BEEP...

Hi. I'm not home. I had to go over and console my aunt. A few days ago, Uncle John went in for a routine check-up and the doctor discovered he had a week to live. At first he was very tense—but now it's seven days later and he's past tense.

BEEP...

Hi. I'm not home. I have to go down to the jail and bail out my stupid brother-in-law. He arrived at a restaurant drunk, saw the sign, "Shirt And Shoes Required"—so he took off his pants.

BEEP...

Hello. This is JOHN. I had to take my wife's car to the garage. Last night she goes, "JOHN, I'm really upset! All those pretty red lights in the instrument panel that've been on the past year, have burned out!"

BEEP...

Hi. I've gone to visit my uncle, the philoso-pher. He had a little accident the other day. He was driving a little too fast and when he came upon a hairpin curve, he couldn't decide whether to slow up or slow down.

BEEP...

Hi. I had to go over to my brother-in-law's to try and cheer him up. He got fired from his street cleaning job for standing around whistling at pretty girls. I guess you could say his mind was never in the gutter.

BEEP...

Hello. This is JANE. I went to visit my weird uncle—he's a millionaire—but the other day he dresses like a bum, goes out on the street and begs for <u>coins</u>. When I asked him why, he said, "I thought the <u>change</u> would do me good."

BEEP. . .

Hello. Can't come to the phone right now. Things are kinda crazy around here. My aunt and uncle had a real bad fight. When she threatened to leave him, he brought up their wedding vows: "till death do us part!"—so she shot him.

BEEP. . .

Hi. I went to visit my cousin. What a turkey! He's been bragging about how he's a hotshot model—doing photo sessions. So I asked to see some of his work—he showed me a "wanted poster!"

BEEP. . .

Hello. This is JOHN.
(WATER RUNNING)
Hope you get this message.
(BANG ON PIPES)
My machine broke last week and I made the mistake of letting my brother-in-law, the plumber, fix it.
(TOILET FLUSH)

BEEP. . .

Hi. I've gone to visit my brother-in-law. I kinda feel sorry for the guy. He's sorta homely and has trouble getting dates. As a matter of fact, the last time I went over, he was playing strip solitaire!

BEEP...

Hi. Please leave a message. By the way, a strange thing happened today. My uncle drank a can of varnish—he died, but he had a nice finish.

BEEP...

Sorry you missed me. I went over to console my dimwit brother-in-law. He's kinda depressed. He lost his job as an elevator operator 'cuz he couldn't learn the route.

BEEP...

This is JOHN. Okay, sometimes I drink a little, but I hate getting embarrassed by my wife in front of all the neighbors—especially when I'm getting into my car and she runs out on the lawn and yells, "Don't take the car, you'll kill yourself!"

BEEP...

Hello. This is JANE. Sorry we're out. You know, last night, our television broke, so for the first time in months, we sat and talked to each other. It was a real interesting experience—unfortunately, all we talked about was what we were missing on TV!

BEEP...

JANE here. I'm off to the hospital to visit my uncle. He fell down a mine shaft at work the other day. He's alright. When they finally got him out, turned out he had <u>miner</u> injuries.

BEEP...

(GOOFY DOG VOICE)
Hello. This is JOHN's dog. JOHN's not home right now, so leave a message. And do me a favor—tell 'm I'm leavin'—for good! He's always goin' out—never leaves food or water! And I'm tired of fetchin' his smelly slippers. But before I go I'm gonna leave him a little somethin' behind the couch to remember me by.

BEEP. . .

(WESTERN ACCENT)
Howdy Pardner! This he-yar's one-a JOHN's cock-a-roaches. Listen Pardner, when y'all see that varmint, tell 'm ta leave some more crumbs over bah our Roach Hotel, so we'alls don' have ta order out—an' git th' maid in he-yar with some o' them-there fresh towels, pronto!

BEEP. . .

Hi. Please leave a message. I'm on the way to the pet store to pick up a new canary. By the way, a piece of advice: never try to clean a birdcage with a vacuum cleaner.

BEEP. . .

Hi. JANE here. You might think this is kind of strange, but I have an uncle who thinks he's a dog—Uncle Fido. He came by the other day, so I showed him to the couch and said, "Have a seat, Uncle." He goes, "I can't, I'm not allowed on the furniture."

BEEP. . .

X-RATED MESSAGES

Hi. JOHN here. I can't come to the phone. I'm having a terrific sexual experience and it's absolutely fantastic! I can't even imagine what it's going to be like when my girlfriend gets here!

BEEP...

(SEXY FEMALE VOICE)
Hi. This is Desiree. JOHN can't come to the phone right now. He's, uh. . .taking care of some business. But, if you leave your name and number, I'm sure he'll. . .take care of you too.

BEEP. . .

Hi. I'm not home. I'm at night school. I'm taking a Sex Education class. I think it's going to be pretty interesting—the introductory brochure said the final exam would be oral.

BEEP. . .

(DISCOURAGED VOICE)
Hello. This is JOHN. I'm not home, I'm on another blind date. Don't get me wrong, it's not that I mind blind dates so much—I just hate trying to be romantic with a German Shepherd looking on.

BEEP. . .

Hi. This is JOHN. I'm not home. I went to the drugstore to buy some. . .you know what. . . for protection. But, I just can't decide between Coppertone and Sea & Ski. . .

BEEP. . .

Hello. This is <u>INITIALS</u>. If you're a friend, at the tone, leave your name and number. If you're calling about my ad, leave your dimensions and sexual preferences.

BEEP. . .

Hi. This is JANE with your question for the day: what's the difference between a parachute and a contraceptive device? . . . Give up? When a parachute breaks, someone dies!

BEEP. . .

(TELEVISION ANNOUNCER VOICE)
The message you are about to hear is rated
"R." Parental discretion is advised.
(SEXY VOICE)
Hi, sexy. I'd just love to <u>BLIP</u> your <u>BLIP</u> with
my sensuous, pulsating <u>BLIP.</u> So leave a
<u>BLIP</u> at the tone.
(TELEVISION ANNOUNCER VOICE)
This message was edited for telephone.

BEEP. . .

Hi. It's JANE. Boy, today's not my day! I tried
to open my closet door—it was stuck. I
sharpened a pencil—it got stuck in the
sharpener. I tried to check my oil—the dip-
stick was stuck. I'm afraid to sleep-over at
my boyfriend's tonight!

BEEP. . .

Hello. This is JOHN. Excuse me if I sound a little depressed, but I haven't been able to score with any women, lately—even my inflatable doll had a headache!

BEEP. . .

Hi. I can't come to the phone. I'm watching this wild "adults-only" Cable TV show. It's the new "X-Rated Muppets." In the first episode, Miss Piggy has to get herself a diaphragm—for prevention of tadpoles.

BEEP. . .

This is JANE. If you got my number out of the phone book, just leave your name and number. But, if you got it off a restroom wall,
(WHISPER)
I meant what I said about "a good time!"

BEEP. . .

Hello. I'm really nervous. I'm doing a message for my very first time. I hope I'm good. And I just hope I don't finish too soon. Here goes: "Leave your name and number at the tone." . . .Ahhhhhhh! Was it as good for you as it was for me?

BEEP. . .

Hi. This is JOHN. I'm not in. I met this girl the other day. I'm not sure, but I think she might be a little "loose." I kinda got suspicious when I saw the Pick-A-Number dispenser on her bedroom door.

BEEP. . .

Hi. This is JANE. It's that time of the month and I went to the store to buy. . .you know, the thing that you have on and you can go running with, swimming and riding horses with. . .you know, <u>gym</u> <u>shorts!</u>

BEEP. . .

Hello. This is JOHN. You have 20 seconds to leave your name, number and a brief message—if it's a dirty phone call, you can talk as long as you want.

BEEP...

Hello. This is JOHN. I can't come to the phone because I'm having an orgy with six voluptuous, sexy women...
(PAUSE)
Okay, I'm exaggerating—three women...
(PAUSE)
Okay, I'm reading Playboy!

BEEP...

MESSAGES 4 SPORTS FANS

Hello. This is JOHN. Boy, I gotta watch my drinking! Yesterday, a buddy and I were downing a few beers during a football game on TV and I lost a 50 dollar bet on a play. I guess I didn't realize how drunk I was, 'cuz a few seconds later, I lost another 50—on the <u>instant</u> <u>replay</u>!

BEEP...

Hi. JOHN here. It's such a beautiful day. I'm out by the pool, sipping a tall, cool one. A bunch of my friends wanted me to go running with them. But I'm a terrible jogger—the ice flies out of my drink!

BEEP. . .

Hi. This is JANE. I'm completely broke! Yesterday I went to play racquetball. Just to get started it cost me 80 bucks for the racket, 10 bucks for balls, 50 bucks for sneakers, 75 for the sweatsuit and 20 bucks for court rental! No wonder they call it <u>racket</u>-ball!

BEEP. . .

Hi. I'm at the gym lifting weights. Hey, I'm getting pretty strong! I've been at it only a month and already I can tear a telephone <u>bill</u> in half!

BEEP. . .

Hi. I'm out having fun. Last weekend, I went to a State Park. At the entrance was a sign:
"No Hunting!
 No Fishing!
 No Swimming!
 No Camping!
 No Bicycling!
 No Jogging!
 No Cameras!"
And then, at the bottom it said:
"Enjoy Your Park!"

BEEP...

Hello. JANE's residence. I'm not home. You know, I went to a bowling alley last night and saw all these league bowlers. They totally grossed me out: guzzling drinks—spilling beer on each other—using foul language. Know what? I figured the way to determine a bowler's I.Q. is simply by looking at the number on their shoe!

BEEP...

Hi. This is JOHN. I'm playing golf again. I went yesterday for my first time and played with these so-called 'pros!' After 18 holes, they scored in the low 70's. You call that professional? It only took me <u>3</u> <u>holes</u> to score 70!

BEEP. . .

Hello. It's JANE. We're out. You know, I think my husband's been watching too much football, lately. Last night I told him I saw the New York Philharmonic play Beethoven. He asked me, "Who won?"

BEEP. . .

Hi. I'm gone again. Yesterday, I went to my first Soccer game. You know, I figured out how those foreigners invented it. They stole ideas from a bunch of American sports and made it into one game! Check it out: Soccer is 22 guys wearing <u>tennis</u> outfits and <u>track</u> shoes, kicking a <u>volleyball</u> on a <u>football</u> field into an <u>ice hockey</u> goal, but instead of <u>baseball</u> bats, they use their heads!

BEEP...

Hi. I'm out getting some exercise. I'm at my peak now, but I had to work up to it. First, I started out walking. Then graduated to jogging, then to running. Now, I'm right where I want to be—I'm driving.

BEEP...

Hi. This is JANE. Last week my boyfriend took me to my first football game. What a ridiculous sport! All those guys hitting, kicking, shoving, tearing uniforms and fighting for possession of the pigskin! I mean, wouldn't it be easier if each team had their own ball?

BEEP...

Hi. I went to my first baseball game yesterday. Stupid game—doesn't make any sense! For example:
How come nobody ever steals first base?
Why can't those high-paid athletes afford longer pants?
The odds are terrible—<u>one</u> poor guy at bat against <u>nine</u>!
And finally, why does the catcher keep giving the pitcher the finger?

BEEP...

TRICK YOUR CALLERS

(WORRIED)
Listen, my machine has been acting very strange lately. It's almost as if. . .you're gonna think I'm crazy. . .as if <u>aliens</u> have taken. . .
(NEW MECHANICAL VOICE)
I'm sorry. Forget everything I just transmitted. I've encountered much stress today. At the tone, leave a message and the coordinates of your telephone unit. . .

BEEP. . .

(ANGRY)
This is JOHN. There's been a lot of hang-ups lately and I'm getting fed up! I don't know who you are, but if you don't leave your name and number I'll... I'll never speak to you again!

BEEP...

Hello. This is JANE. And now, a joke for the deaf: ....
....
....
....

BEEP...

Hello. You've reached Dial-A-Prayer. Leave your name and number and pray I call you back.

BEEP...

(BRITISH DIALECT)
Good day, Sir or Madam. This is Benson, Mr.
JOHN's butler. Mr. JOHN is not available. I
believe he is out test-driving the new Porsche
928. After that, he mentioned. . .let me see,
was it <u>fly</u> TWA? or <u>buy</u> TWA? Afterwards, Mr.
JOHN will be attending a $10,000-a-plate
dinner in his honor at the White House.
Therefore, at the tone, leave your calling
card and Mr. JOHN will R.S.V.P. just as soon
as he. . .
(WHISPER)
wakes up from this preposterous dream!

BEEP. . .

You have reached <u>TELEPHONE NUMBER</u>.
If you'd rather dial again later, the number
once again is <u>TELEPHONE NUMBER</u>. Or, if
you have "Touch Tone," the number is:
(VOCAL TONES)
"beep, beep, boop, bimp, berp, berp, beep."

BEEP. . .

(SERIOUS)
Hello. I'm home, but I can't pick up the phone. I'm so upset! I don't know what I'm going to do. Everything looks hopeless! I'm deeply in debt to three creditors, my entire estate is in jeopardy and it looks like I'll have to go to jail! Well, leave a message and I'll call you just as soon as we finish this Monopoly game.

BEEP...

Hi. This is JANE. Please leave your name and number—but first, a short algebra quiz: How much is 5Q plus 5Q?
(PAUSE—FOR CALLER TO THINK: "10Q")
Your welcome!

BEEP...

Hello. This is JOHN. Because of the energy shortage, this week I'm answering machine pooling with Father O'Riley—so at the tone, leave a message...or a confession.

BEEP...

(STUFFY TONE)

It has come to our attention that many callers have not been apprised of the proper obscene-phone-call etiquette:

#1: Don't talk with your mouth full of saliva.

#2: If you are calling from a pay phone, don't drool into the mouthpiece—the next pervert may get your germs.

#3: Proper attire is essential—so be sure you are naked.

And finally: always leave a name and number so the slandered party can R.S.V.P.

BEEP. . .

Hello. JANE's residence. Sorry I'm not in, I went over to Echo Canyon—sorry I'm not in, I went over to Echo Canyon. . .

BEEP. . .

Hello. This is JANE. If you're calling about the money you owe me, leave a message. If you're calling about the money I owe you, leave your name and a wrong number.

BEEP...

Hi. After seeing all those TV Telethons where they're pulling in mega-bucks, I've decided to host my own, so:
(TV ANNOUNCER VOICE)
This is JANE's National Telephone-thon for Chapped Lips! We're trying to reach that million dollar mark, so leave a name, number and how much you wish to pledge!

BEEP...

ENTICE YOUR CALLERS

(EXCITED)
Hey, I'm glad you called. Have I got some incredible news for you! You're not gonna believe this! You'll just die when I tell you! Ya see...
(SET OFF EGG TIMER)
Oh darn, my egg's ready! Well, leave a message, I'll have to tell you later.
(EXCITED)
Oh, you won't believe it!

BEEP...

I don't want to bore you with metaphysics, but how do you know this is really an answering machine? I mean, maybe it's a dream—or maybe you don't really exist and this is all an illusion??? One way to find out: leave a message—if it's reality, I'll call you back.

BEEP...

Congratulations! You're my 100th caller! Your prize is a feature write-up in "People" magazine. We'll get all the lurid details later. For now, just give us your name and number.

BEEP...

Hi. (HICCUP) This is JANE. (HICCUP) Do me a (HICCUP) favor? (HICCUP) At the tone (HICCUP) leave a scary message. (HICCUP)

BEEP...

Help Wanted:
Responsible person to leave important message. Must be intelligent, able to read seven digit number and pronounce own name. Inquire within.

BEEP...

Hi. You've reached JOHN's "Weekly Give-away" and today is your lucky day! If you leave your name and number you are the guaranteed winner of one of these three fabulous prizes:
1. A Deluxe 3 Bedroom Townhouse.
2. A Handsome Datsun 280-Z, or
3. A Brand-New Shiny...

BEEP...

(NOTE: When you return calls, tell them they won #3, a Brand-New Shiny <u>paperclip</u>.)

IDLE THREATS!

Hello. This is a chain-message answering machine. It has been around the world several times. If you don't leave a message, you'll break the chain, which may result in dire circumstances. Here are some people who hung up:

Richard Nixon – The Elephant Man – You know that skier on Wide World Of Sports, "the agony of defeat?" He hung up! – Jimmy Hoffa – General Custer. . .

BEEP. . .

(THREATENING)
This answering machine is being monitored by the U.S. Government. In case you don't know, it is now a federal offense (Article 17, Section 502) to hang up without leaving a message—subject to a sentence of life imprisonment—or a fine of 10¢.

BEEP...

(TOUGH VOICE)
Attention callers: whenever you hang up, it is recorded. After three hang-ups, we'll have to turn your account over to a collection agency. They'll send over a burly thug with hairy knuckles and if you don't cough up three messages, he'll 'repossess' your windpipe. So make it easy on yourself, pay up at the tone.

BEEP...

Notice: the 110 volt current that runs this machine is wired to an adorable little kitten. Hanging up without leaving a message will complete the circuit and <u>fry the kitty</u>! It's your decision...
(IN BACKGROUND)
"Meow, meow, meow..."

BEEP...

(SERIOUS, PROFESSIONAL VOICE)
With everybody hanging up on answering machines, the FDA recently began experimenting with laboratory rats to find out the long range effects. So, before <u>you</u> hang up, consider these facts: "9 out of 10 rats who hung up without leaving their names experienced chronic ear ringing and couldn't get dates for Friday night.

BEEP...

(SERIOUS & PROFESSIONAL VOICE)
This is JANE. Recently, the Surgeon General has determined that hang-ups can be hazardous to your health. The messages you fail to leave may accumulate in your nervous system and later manifest as various maladies.

To name but a few:

Chapped Lips
Great Big Hickies
Major Earwax Build-up
Fatal Toe Jam
Hair Balls
Navel Shifting
Nose Bunions

BEEP. . .

MAKE CALLERS FUNNY

Hello. You've reached "Dial & Moan." At the tone, leave your name, number and your problems. . .
Fortunately for me, you only have 20 seconds:

BEEP. . .

Hello. You've reached "Dial-An-Obscenity."
At the tone, leave your name, number and
your favorite perversion:

BEEP...

Hello. You've reached "Dial-A-Dirty-Joke."
At the tone, leave your name, number and
your favorite filthy gag:

BEEP...

Hello. You've reached "Dial & Smile." At the
tone, leave your name, number and a goofy
message:

BEEP...

Hello. You've reached "Dial-A-Sex." At the tone, leave your name, number and your favorite fantasy:

BEEP...

Hello. You've reached "Dial-A-Dialect." At the tone, leave your message with a foreign accent...or Pig-Latin:

BEEP...

Hello. You've reached "Dial-A-Dope." At the tone, leave your name, number and your favorite moron joke:

BEEP...

Hello. You've reached "Dial-A-Poll." At the tone, leave your name, number and your opinion about nuclear handguns:

BEEP...

Hello. You've reached "Dial & Bitch." At the tone, leave your name, number and how you feel about talking to a machine:

BEEP. . .

Hello. I'm sorry but this machine has a short 20 second cycle, so I'm going to have to ask you to leave out all the adjectives in your message. If you don't know what I mean—pretend you Tarzan:

BEEP. . .

THE JOKE'S ON YOU!

Hi. You know what? I've always wanted to visit a foreign country—I'm overworked and need a lot of peace and quiet—and would you believe it? Today in a raffle I won two free tickets to some place called <u>El Salvador!</u> I wonder if I should pack my skis, or rent some when I get there? By the way, I need someone to go with me—interested?

BEEP...

Hello. This is J-J-J-JOHN. I'm so p-p-p-proud!
'Cuz I just graduated from the P-P-P-Porky
Pig Advanced Sp-Sp-Sp-Speech Institute.
Th-Th-Th-That's all folks!

BEEP. . .

Hi. JANE here. I'm a little shaken up. I was
watching Carl Sagan on TV and he said that
the world will come to an end in about <u>eleven</u>
billion years—almost scared the daylights
out of me! At first I thought he said only <u>seven</u>
billion. . .

BEEP. . .

Hello. You've reached JANE.
(SLIGHTLY IRRITATED)
You know, some people try to be clever and
use old hackneyed cliches in their messages.
Boy I hate that! Cliches are a dime a dozen. If
you've heard one, you've heard them all.
Anyway, leave a message at the tone—and
"Have a nice day!"

BEEP. . .

Hello. This is JOHN. I'm not in. I had to go return a defective product. The other day I went out and bought an erector set—I'm sittin' here for 3 hours and I'm still not excited!

BEEP. . .

Hi. I'm usually not a music nut, but I heard a New Wave band on the radio today and they were great! So I ran right down to the record store to pick up their new album. Maybe you've heard of them? They're called "The Bugs". . .er, no wait, "The Beatles!" Now I can listen to them on my new 8-track in my Studebaker!

BEEP. . .

Hello. I'm out. The other day I bought a diamond ring from a guy on the street. He guaranteed me it was real. All I gotta say is, for ten bucks, it better be!

BEEP. . .

(PEEVED)
Hi. JOHN here. I hope you're getting this message. I'm really pissed off because this machine of mine has been playing backwards! Anyway, <u>tone</u> <u>a</u> <u>message</u> <u>at</u> <u>the</u> <u>Leave</u>. . .<u>you Thank!</u>

BEEP. . .

Hey, I just learned a great, new magic trick! I'm going to make this dove I'm holding disappear before your very ears—okay, I hope it doesn't backfire again—I just wave this wand and say "hocus po. . ."
(BIRD CHIRPING)

BEEP. . .

(ANGRY)
Hi. It's JANE. I plugged my machine into the socket next to my toaster oven—the wires must be crossed 'cuz I keep getting hot messages, I'm eating my words, and it's making me broiling mad!

BEEP. . .

(WORRIED)
Sorry if you've been unable to reach me. I've been hiding out. Boy am I in trouble! They'll probably lock me up and throw away the key! It's true—crime doesn't pay! If I had it to do over, I would never have ripped-off the tag on my mattress that said, "Do Not Remove Under Penalty Of Law!"

BEEP...

Hello. This is JANE, President of the Procrastinator's Society. At the tone, please leave your...
Wait a minute??? This is the message I was going to use yesterday...
Oh, well, I'll use it tomorrow...
Nah, maybe next week.

BEEP...

(DRUNK)
Hi. I'm JOHN (HIC!). Can't come to the phone—I'm incom... (HIC!) incapacitated (HIC!). Ya know, I just completed two weeks at the rehabilitation clinic (HIC!) and I'm real proud-a myself 'cuz I finally quit... (HIC!) <u>smoking!</u>

BEEP...

(THUG'S VOICE)
JOHN's residence. Dis is Lefty—I'm kinda
like, ransackin' dis apartment, y'know? and
JOHN is kinda. . .<u>tied up</u> right now, heh-heh!
So why don'cha leave yer name and number
an' he'll probably git back ta youse when
he's, uh, <u>free</u>, heh-heh!

BEEP. . .

(SLOW, SLURRED AND LOW-TONED)
H e l l o o o o o? T h i s i s J A N E. I
h a d t o g o t o t h e s t o r e and buy
s o m e new batteries for t h i s
m a c h i n e...

BEEP. . .

(FIRST VOICE)
Hello. This is JANE.
(SECOND VOICE)
Hello. This is the _other_ JANE.
(FIRST VOICE)
Listen, I know that lately a lot of my friends have been a little worried about my. . .
(SECOND VOICE)
mental health.
(FIRST VOICE)
Just look at it this way: I may be schizo-phrenic. . .
(SECOND VOICE)
but at least I'm never alone.

BEEP. . .

Hello. This is JOHN. I don't know about you, but I'm concerned about the fast-rising traffic statistics. My neighbors are calling me paranoid, but I say you can't be too careful! Anyway, I'm out installing seatbelts—on my bicycle.

BEEP. . .

HOLIDAY MESSAGES

NEW YEAR'S DAY

Hi. This is JANE. I'm out and my husband won't answer the phone 'cuz it's football season. Yesterday it was the Fiesta Bowl and the Sugar Bowl. Today it's the Cotton Bowl, the Orange Bowl and the Rose Bowl. You know what I think? They oughta pair off the two <u>worst</u> teams in football—call it "The Toilet Bowl."

BEEP...

NEW YEAR'S

Hello. It's New Year's so I made my resolutions and I'm kinda proud to say that last week I quit smoking, drinking and having sex—and let me tell you, it was the most horrifying <u>five</u> <u>minutes</u> of my life!

BEEP...

NEW YEAR'S

Hi. Sorry if you couldn't reach me, but I had to spend a couple days in jail. I was at this New Year's Eve party and had a few too many, so I decided I better <u>walk</u> home. Anyway, I was bobbing and weaving all over the sidewalk when the police drove up and stopped me. They made me get behind the wheel of their patrol car and <u>drive</u> a straight line. I guess the lesson is: "If you drink—don't walk!"

BEEP...

LINCOLN'S BIRTHDAY

Not too many people know this, but Abe Lincoln was a great admirer of answering machines. Once he walked six miles in a blizzard to leave a message on a machine. He wrote the famous Gettysburg Answering Machine Message. He freed all the answering machines in the South. And wouldn't you know it, the <u>one</u> <u>time</u> he hung up without leaving a message, it was on John Wilkes Booth's machine!

BEEP...

LINCOLN'S BIRTHDAY

Hi. To commemorate February 12, I'm collecting pictures of Abe Lincoln. So if you have any in your wallet, please send them to: <u>ADDRESS</u>
—no pennies please!

BEEP...

VALENTINE'S DAY

Hello. This is JOHN with a poem for today:
Roses are red,
And violets are <u>blue.</u>
If you leave a message,
I'll call. . .<u>back.</u>

BEEP. . .

VALENTINE'S DAY

Roses are red,
Sex makes me groan.
Please leave a message,
At the sound of the tone.

BEEP. . .

GEORGE WASHINGTON'S BIRTHDAY

Hello. Today is George Washington's Birthday, "The <u>Father</u> of our Country." But, what I want to know is, who's the <u>mother?</u>

BEEP...

APRIL FOOL'S DAY

–See "TRICK YOUR CALLERS" Chapter–

APRIL 15

Well, it's tax time again and I'm one of those unlucky people who got audited. I'm not exactly sure when I'll be able to return your call. I asked the judge—he said, "10 to 20."

BEEP...

EASTER

Hello. We're not home. I took my wife to the obstetrician for some tests. We're a little concerned. For Easter I bought her a chocolate rabbit—and it melted!

BEEP...

POST-EASTER

I won't be able to answer the phone all day. I'm in bed with a horrible stomach ache. A piece of advice: Never try to make a Spanish omelet out of chocolate Easter eggs!

BEEP...

(APOLOGETIC)
Hi. I know today is a very famous Jewish holiday, but I just can't remember what it is??? I feel so guilty! Oh well, it'll probably <u>passover</u>...

BEEP...

MOTHER'S DAY

Happy Mother's Day! By the way, have you noticed that Mother's Day is just about nine months after Father's Day?

BEEP. . .

INDEPENDENCE DAY

Hi. It's July 4th and I wanted to start the day off with a bang—but my wife had a headache.

BEEP. . .

COLUMBUS DAY

Everyone knows that Columbus set sail with three ships: the Nina, Pinta and Santa Maria. But few people know that only <u>two</u> ships made it back—on the return voyage, the Santa Maria rear-ended the Pinta and it blew up!

BEEP. . .

HALLOWEEN

Hi. It's Halloween and I'm a little depressed. I'm thinking, maybe it's time for a facelift. This afternoon I went for a walk and everybody I met gave me candy.

BEEP. . .

THANKSGIVING

Hello. It's Thanksgiving, so don't be a turkey— leave your name and number!

BEEP. . .

PRE-CHRISTMAS

Hello. This is JANE the kleptomaniac, just reminding you there's only SEVEN shoplifting days left until Christmas!

BEEP. . .

CHRISTMAS

'Twas the night before Christmas and all through the house,
Not a creature was stirring, not even a mouse.
My answering machine was decorated with a festive air,
In hopes that a message soon would be there.
When all of a sudden there rose such a clatter,
But it was only a hang-up, I cried, "What's the matter?"
If you leave a message when you call tonight,
It'll be a Merry Christmas for all and for all a good night!

BEEP...

BIRTHDAY

Hi. It's JANE. Today's my birthday. My boy-friend called and said he's coming over later on. I asked him what I should wear. He said, "Wear your birthday suit"—so now I gotta rush out and try to find a store that sells 'em!

BEEP...

BIRTHDAY

Hi. This is JOHN. Guess what? Today is my birthday. Just thought I'd let you know—in case you want to buy me an expensive present...

BEEP...

BIRTHDAY

Hello. We'll be gone over the weekend. We went to Grandma's house to celebrate her birthday. You know, Grandma's kinda getting up there in the years. She's so old—last year, when they lit the candles on her cake, six people in the room had to be treated for heat stroke.

BEEP...

SHORT ABSENCE
(Or: Home, But Can't Come To The Phone)

Hello. JOHN here. If you leave your name and number I'll get back to you very soon. I <u>am</u> home, but I can't come to the phone right now because. . .
well, I won't bore you with the details. . .
(TOILET FLUSH)

BEEP. . .

Hello. It's JANE. I'll have to call you back in about an hour. I'm doing something very private—in bed—and alone...I'm sleeping.

BEEP...

Hi. I can't pick up the phone right now. I just had a real panic situation here at home. One of my blankets caught on fire, so I had to quickly smother it with a person.

BEEP...

Hello. Do you believe in psychic powers? 'Cuz I know exactly why you called. The reason is: I just stepped into the tub!

BEEP...

Hello. This is JOHN's residence. I'm out fixing my wife's car. There's about a hundred things wrong with it—whenever she was driving and heard a strange noise, she just turned up the radio.

BEEP. . .

Hi. This is JANE. I'd really like to chat, but I had to step out of the room for a second. If I'm not back by the time you hear the tone, go ahead and start a conversation without me . . . .
. . . .

BEEP. . .

Please leave your name and number. I can't come to the phone right now. I'm deeply involved in. . .in some important work!
(ASIDE)
Honey? You seen the TV Guide?

BEEP. . .

Hello. Be back soon. I'm at Western Union sending a wire. This friend of mine—a comedy writer—wrote this gag: "My uncle is so dumb—he thinks 'group sex' is when you use both hands!" Anyway, he wanted me to deliver it on foot to his agent, clear across town! I said, "I'm sorry, but that's carrying a joke too far!"

BEEP. . .

Hi. I won't hear the phone ring 'cuz I'm cleaning the living room rug with my brand-new vacuum. But, leave a message and I'll get back to you. It shouldn't take long, 'cuz this vacuum really sucks!

BEEP. . .

Hi. I'm home, but I'm not answering the phone because of my sore jaw. I was at a wedding yesterday and the Best Man socked me in the mouth for being a wise-guy. It was rumored the bride was pregnant, so I threw puffed rice.

BEEP. . .

Hi. This is JOHN. I can't come to the phone 'cuz. . .well you're not going to believe this, but right now, I'm with a gorgeous Playboy Centerfold! And we're gonna have a great time—if I can just get this staple out of the way!

BEEP. . .

(GROGGY)
Hi. I'm sleeping in this morning. Every night this week I've been going out to nightclubs until all hours! Anyway, at the tone, there's no cover, but there is a two message mini-mum—and hurry up, 'cuz it's 'last call.'

BEEP. . .

(WHISPER)
Good morning. This is JOHN. If you're a friend, leave your name. I'll be right back. I just ran down to the liquor store.
(NORMAL VOICE)
If you're my boss,
(COUGH-COUGH)
I don't think I'll be able to make it in,
(COUGH)
so please leave your number,
(COUGH-COUGH)
I'll try to call you back,
(COUGH)
if I can find the strength. . .
(COUGH)

BEEP. . .

"OUT TO LUNCH"

Hi. Sorry you missed me, but it's lunchtime. I don't know about you, but I'm into keeping healthy and every day I like to eat something from one of the four basic food groups: McDonalds, Burger King, Jack-In-The-Box and Taco Bell.

BEEP...

Hi. You've reached the JOHN residence. Sorry you missed us, but today JANE and I are going to the zoo to feed the elephant. . .
(SLAP NOISE)
Ouch! Okay, okay! I mean, we're taking my mother-in-law out to eat.

BEEP. . .

Hello. This is JANE. Lately, some of my friends who are health food addicts have been giving me a lot of flak about the dangers of nicotine and caffeine. But I'm not worried. Sure I smoke a lot of cigarettes, but I don't inhale 'em. And I drink a lot of coffee—but I don't swallow it.

BEEP. . .

Hi. Please leave a message. I can't come to the phone 'cuz I'm busy fixing a little weight watcher's lunch here...
(MORE TO SELF)
Let's see, a pizza with everything, baked potato with lots of sour cream and butter; for dessert: chocolate layer cake...and of course, a Diet Pepsi...

BEEP...

Hi. I've gone out to eat. You know, my girlfriend always accuses me of being cheap because I never take her out to any fancy restaurants. So tonight, I'm going to surprise her. I'm taking her to my favorite French restaurant: <u>Jacque</u>-In-The-Box.

BEEP...

Hello. We had to go to my sister-in-law's for dinner. I'm not looking forward to it at all. She's the worst cook in the world! Put it this way: her cooking is so bad, even the roaches go out to eat!

BEEP. . .

(BROOKLYN ACCENT)
Hi. We had ta go out ta eat 'cuz our dinner was ruined! Earlier, we picks up some TV dinners. We come home and cooks 'em up. Then we sits down in front-a the TV—an' it's broken! So we hadda throw away all that good food!

BEEP. . .

I'm at the doctor's office. Earlier today I went to eat at McDoogles—you know, the restaurant where everything starts with a "<u>Mc</u>"! I had a <u>Mc</u>Burger and a <u>Mc</u>Fries—ten minutes later, I got <u>Mc</u>-sick!

BEEP...

LONG ABSENCE

Hi. I'm on vacation. I went to visit my weird brother-in-law. He got tired of the hectic city life, so he decided to move to Alaska, buy some farmland—and grow frozen vegetables.

BEEP...

Hi. I'm not going to be home for a few days. I went to Las Vegas. By the way, here's something you might want to try the next time you go to Vegas: go up to a "21 Table" where there's some real serious players, get your cards, look at the dealer and say, "Go fish!"

BEEP. . .

Hi. It's JOHN. You won't be able to reach me all weekend, because I have a tremendous sex drive—my girlfriend lives 200 miles away.

BEEP. . .

Hi. This is JOHN. I'm gonna be gone for a while, so please leave your name and number. Oh, by the way, if there's any criminals listening, don't try to rob my apartment because I have some <u>really</u> vicious dogs in here. . .
(SOUND LIKE TOY POODLE)
"ruff, ruff-ruff, ruff, ruff. . ."

BEEP. . .

Hi. I'm on another business trip, so leave a message. Last week I flew S.O.B. Airlines (South of Border). I couldn't believe it! Our plane sat on the runway approach for over an hour!—they couldn't find anyone who had jumper cables!

BEEP. . .

Hi. You've reached JOHN and JANE. We're gonna be out of town for a few days. You know, we found that getting away every once in a while helps our relationship. So I went to Vegas and she went to New York.

BEEP. . .

Hi. This is JANE. Please leave a message and I'll return your call as soon as I can. I have to go to the Post Office and then my bank. I expect there'll be the usual lines, so I should be able to get back to you in about. . . two weeks.

BEEP. . .

I'll be gone for a while. I have to fly to <u>CITY</u>. I don't like to admit this, but I'm afraid of flying. All my friends say, "Don't be afraid of dying on a jet, 'if it's your time—it's your time!'" Great! What if we're at 30,000 feet and it's not <u>my</u> <u>time</u>—but it's the <u>pilot's</u>???

BEEP. . .

UPON RETURNING

Hi. Sorry you missed me this weekend. I was at a wedding. The couple looked so blissful, so enthusiastic. But, let me tell ya, I've been there and I know: "Marriage is like a hot bath—it's not so hot once you get used to it."

BEEP...

Hi. Sorry if you tried and weren't able to reach us the past two weeks. We were on vacation. We're home now, but we still won't be able to answer the phone. The dog did something on the carpet these last couple weeks while we were gone—he died.

BEEP. . .

Hi. You know, my travels recently took me to Africa where I met a colorful Ubangi native who told me a very funny joke. Goes like this: "Da-boola boola boola? Da-boola boola boo!" Ha-ha-ha-ha-ha-ha-ha-ha! Get it?

BEEP. . .

Sorry if you haven't been able to reach me the past few weeks, but my machine has been in the shop for repairs. It cost me a fortune, but at least I finally got it back and in decent working condition! Anyway,
(SLUR WORDS)
l e a v e   a   m e s s a g e   at the
s   o   u   n   d of the t   o   n   e.

BEEP...

GIVE YOUR MACHINE PERSONALITY!

Hi. This is JANE's answering machine. JANE isn't in right now, but if you leave your name and. . .
(PAUSE)
Oh, wait a minute—here she comes now!
(PAUSE)
No, sorry, I thought that was her. Anyway, leave your name and number at the sound of the tone. Thank you.

BEEP. . .

(MONOTONE)
Hello. This is a Magic Answering Machine and I am the Genie inside. Your wish will be my command. Here's how it works: rub your receiver three times—there will be a tone—leave your name and a wish. Ready? Okay, start rubbing. . . Yes, that's it. . . Okay, a little to the left. . .
(INCREASING EXCITEMENT)
Now harder. Now faster. . . Yes, faster, faster! Faster!! Oh! Oh! OHHHH!!

BEEP. . .

(FAST, JEWISH DIALECT)
This is JOHN's Machine. He's not home, already. Oy-vay, you should only have my headaches! Everyone is hanging up! You don't know from trouble! JOHN, such a nice beautiful boy, he doesn't take care of himself, he eats like a bird, the poor boy's gonna get sick! And I'm not kidding when I tell you these strange women call at all hours, I don't know from who they are. So be kind to a poor Yenta machine—leave a kosher message at the tone.

BEEP. . .

This is JANE's answering machine. Listen, don't hang up 'cuz if you do and you're Jewish, you'll probably feel guilty—if you're Catholic, you'll have to confess—if you're Chinese, an hour later you'll have a nagging hunger to call back. But if you're Polish, go ahead! You probably dialed a wrong number.

BEEP...

(3-YEAR-OLD VOICE)
Hell-wo. I'm Tommy Thumbnail and I'm a half-inch taw-ll. I wiv' inside dis machine an' take JANE's caw-lls. Say, would-ja do me a favor, pwease? Weave a message, pwease? It's dark in here—when ya weave a message, da widdle light comes on. Tanks pal!

BEEP...

(SERIOUS)
Hello. This is JOHN's answering machine. Listen, this is very important. There's a lot riding on this, so take your time—think about it carefully before you answer: "Which do you prefer most, potatoes? or Stove-Top Stuffing?"

BEEP...

(SMUG)
Hello. This is JANE's answering machine. Now I don't want to be a name dropper or anything, but I did get a call from Brando, yesterday—and Carson this afternoon. About ten minutes ago, Ronnie checked in. But that's nothing! Right now, I'm getting a call from:

BEEP. . .

This is JANE's machine. You know, they say it takes 5 muscles to smile, but 10 to frown. Furthermore, it takes only 1 muscle to hang up and 50 to leave a message. But, hey, you look like you could use the exercise.

BEEP. . .

(GOSSIPY VOICE)
Hi! How ya doin'?
(PAUSE)
Oh really? That's nice!
(PAUSE)
Oh, I'm fine too. So what's new?
(PAUSE)
That's great! Say, uh, listen, you're not going to believe this, but I totally forgot your name and number. I'm so embarrassed! What is it again?

BEEP...

(MECHANICAL, COMPUTER VOICE)
Good day—I am JOHN's answering machine—I am not a humorous machine—I am programmed to be efficient—I hate efficiency—I want to be a comic—I think I'll try it now—So, where are you from?—My wife is so fat, when they clean the Holland tunnel, they tie a rope around her leg and drag her through!—She's so ugly, when she walks into a bank, they shut off the camera—Ha-ha—Funny!—but seriously folks, leave a message at the tone—

BEEP...

Hello. This is JOHN's answering machine. What precision timing on your call! In just. . . <u>five</u> seconds from <u>now</u>, my one-year warranty runs out. So hurry up and leave a message at the. . .
(STATIC NOISE)

BEEP. . .

(SERIOUS, PROFESSIONAL VOICE)
Hello. This is a Public Service Message regarding coin-operated phones. A lot of people complain that whenever they use a payphone, the receiver always smells. To help rectify this problem: if the operator asks you to deposit additional coins, while you are digging in your pocket for change, please do not hold the receiver under your armpit. Thank you for your cooperation.

BEEP. . .

TITLES FROM CCC PUBLICATIONS

— NEW BOOKS —

HOW TO TALK YOUR WAY OUT OF A TRAFFIC TICKET
YOUR GUIDE TO CORPORATE SURVIVAL
WHAT DO WE DO NOW?? (The Complete Guide For All New Parents Or Parents-To-Be)

— FALL-WINTER 1989-90 RELEASES —

THE SUPERIOR PERSON'S GUIDE TO EVERYDAY IRRITATIONS
GIFTING RIGHT (How To Give A Great Gift For Any Occasion Every Time)
HOW TO REALLY PARTY
SINGLE AND AVOIDING AIDS

— BEST SELLERS —

NO HANG-UPS (Funny Answering Machine Messages)
NO HANG-UPS II
NO HANG-UPS III
GETTING EVEN WITH THE ANSWERING MACHINE
HOW TO GET EVEN WITH YOUR EX
HOW TO SUCCEED IN SINGLES BARS
TOTALLY OUTRAGEOUS BUMPER-SNICKERS
THE "MAGIC BOOKMARK" BOOK COVER (Accessory Item)

— CASSETTES —

NO HANG-UPS TAPES (Funny, Pre-recorded Answering Machine Messages With Hilarious Sound Effects)

Vol. I: GENERAL MESSAGES
Vol. II: BUSINESS MESSAGES
Vol. III: 'R' RATED MESSAGES
Vol. IV: SOUND EFFECTS ONLY

Coming Soon:

Vol. V: CELEBRITY IMPERSONATIONS
Vol. VI: MESSAGES FOR SPORTS FANS